D0120174

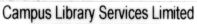

THE WARS
OF FORMER
YUGOSLAVIA

DAVID TAYLOR

www.heinemann.co.uk
Visit our website to find out more information about **Heinemann Library** books.

To order:
  Phone 44 (0) 1865 888066
   Send a fax to 44 (0) 1865 314091
  Visit the Heinemann Bookshop at www.heinemann.co.uk to browse our catalogue
   and order online.

First published in Great Britain by Heinemann Library, Halley Court, Jordan Hill, Oxford
OX2 8EJ, a division of Reed Educational and Professional Publishing Ltd.
Heinemann is a registered trademark of Reed Educational and Professional Publishing Ltd.

OXFORD MELBOURNE AUCKLAND JOHANNESBURG BLANTYRE GABORONE
IBADAN PORTSMOUTH (NH) USA CHICAGO

Designed by AMR
Illustrated by Chartwell Illustrators
Originated by Dot Gradations
Printed by South China Printers

05 04 03 02 01
10 9 8 7 6 5 4 3 2 1
ISBN 0 431 11863 9

British Library Cataloguing in Publication Data

Taylor, David, 1945 July 10-
  The wars of former Yugoslavia. – (Troubled world)
  1.Yugoslavia – History – 1992- – Juvenile literature
  2.Yugoslavia – Politics and government – 1992- – Juvenile literature
  I.Title
  949.7'103

Acknowledgements
The publishers would like to thank the following for permission to reproduce photographs:
Pg.6 Hulton Getty; Pg.7 Bettman/Corbis; Pg.8 Mary Evans Picture Library; Pg.11 Mary Evans
Picture Library; Pg.12 Imperial War Museum; Pg.13 Hulton Deutsch; Pg.14 Imperial War
Museum; Pg.17 Popperfoto; Pg.19 Camera Press/Ivan Meacci; Pg.21 Rex Features; Pg.23 Rex
Features; Pg.25 Rex Features; Pg.26 Popperfoto/Peter Northall; Pg.28 Rex Features; Pg.29 Frank
Spooner; Pg.31 Corbis/Dean Conger; Pg.33 Sipa Press/Rex Features; Pg.34 Rex Features; Pg.36
Popperfoto; Pg.37 Rex Features; Pg.38 Rex Features; Pg.39 Frank Spooner; Pg.40 Topham
Picturepoint/ D Longstreath; Pg.43 Popperfoto/Reuters; Pg.44 Hulton Getty/Kevin Weaver; Pg.45
Rex Features; Pg.46 Rex Features; Pg.47 Rex Features; Pg.48 Popperfoto/Reuters; Pg.49
Popperfoto/Reuters; Pg.50 Camera Press/Viennareport; Pg.51 Popperfoto/Reuters; Pg.53 BBC
News; Pg.54 Centre for the Study of Cartoons and Caricatures, University of Kent; Pg.57
Popperfoto/Reuters; Pg.58 Popperfoto/Reuters; Pg.59 Rex Features.

Cover photograph reproduced with permission of Camera Press.

Every effort has been made to contact copyright holders of any material reproduced in this
book. Any omissions will be rectified in subsequent printings if notice is given to the publishers.

Contents

Words that appear in the text in bold, **like this**, are explained in the glossary.

Yugoslavia and the world

The countries that make up former Yugoslavia are situated in the Balkans, an area of southeast Europe, bordered by the Adriatic and Mediterranean Seas to the west and by the Aegean and Black Seas to the east. The Balkan region is made up of mountains interspersed with fertile plains. To the north the river Danube separates the Balkans from the rest of Europe.

The Balkan Peninsula has always been an important region in history. It is here that the continents of Europe and Asia meet. For over five hundred years the area was under the control of the **Ottoman** and **Habsburg Empires**. Their influence is still in evidence today.

During the 19th century the Ottoman Empire weakened and this caused the great powers of Britain, Austria-Hungary and Russia to take a special interest in the region. They were all concerned about what would happen if the Ottoman Empire, 'the sick man of Europe', lost control of the areas over which it ruled. The Balkans became a hotbed of political intrigue that culminated in the assassination of Archduke Franz Ferdinand, the heir to the Austrian throne. This event sparked off the First World War in June 1914.

The end of the war in 1918 saw the break up of both the Ottoman and Habsburg Empires. Out of the ruins emerged the new country of Yugoslavia, a land that was populated by a mix of peoples, most of whom were descended from the Southern Slavs.

Yugoslavia: What's in a name?
Between 1918 and 1992 the country had three different names:
1918–29: The Kingdom of Serbs, Croats and Slovenes
1929–45: Yugoslavia
1945–92: The Socialist **Federal** Republic of Yugoslavia.

Population:	23,410,000
Area:	250,800 sq km
Capital:	Belgrade (1,470,073)
Languages:	Serbo-Croat, Macedonian, Slovene
Religions:	Orthodox 41%, Roman Catholic 32% Muslim 12%

| Head of State: | President Janez Drnovsek |
| Head of Government: | Ante Markovic |

Ethnic groups
- Serbs and Montenegrins
- Croats
- Muslims
- Slovenes
- Macedonians
- Albanians
- Hungarians
- Bulgarians
- Romanians, Slavs

0   160 km
0   100 miles

Yugoslavia and the Balkan region in 1991.

The Socialist Federal Republic of Yugoslavia in 1991. The large map shows the six republics that make up Yugoslavia and the different groups of people who lived there.

Yugoslavia and the international community

Between 1945 and 1992 Yugoslavia was a **communist** country. From 1945 until 1980 Josip Broz Tito, a determined and single-minded man, led the country. In 1948 Tito quarrelled with Stalin, the leader of the **USSR**. Tito told Stalin that, unlike the other communist countries of Eastern Europe, he would not allow Yugoslavia to be a Soviet **satellite** under the control of Moscow. During the years of the **Cold War**, the western powers, such as the USA and Britain, were happy to help Tito. They saw it as a way of driving a wedge into the communist world and of embarrassing the USSR. As a result, military aid and loans were made available to Tito's government, and Yugoslavia enjoyed a period of relative prosperity.

The British Prime Minister, James Callaghan, greets President Tito of Yugoslavia outside 10 Downing Street, London, 1978.

By the beginning of 1990 this state of affairs no longer existed. Tito died in 1980 and this left a power vacuum that was filled by politicians with **nationalist** agendas who wished to see the break up of Yugoslavia into independent **republics**. Then in 1989 communism collapsed in Eastern Europe and the Cold War came to an end. All of a sudden many people assumed that the world had become a safer place. But they were mistaken.

The break up of Yugoslavia began in 1991 with wars in Slovenia and Croatia. As Yugoslavia was no longer of any use to the West in waging the Cold War there was a sense of complacency among western leaders. They were slow to see what was happening and certainly reluctant to intervene militarily in Yugoslavia. By 1992 Bosnia was plunged into war and the Yugoslavia set up by Tito in 1945 ceased to exist. Only now did the international community get more fully involved. The **European Community (EC)** and **United Nations (UN)** worked to stop the fighting and keep the various sides apart. When the conflict in Kosovo erupted in 1999 the international community acted more swiftly. After the failure of peace talks, the North Atlantic Treaty Organization **(NATO)** carried out a bombing campaign in an effort to bring an end to the conflict.

Who was to blame?

Many people have claimed that the wars of former Yugoslavia were caused by hatred between the various ethnic groups of people that went back for centuries. The truth, however, is not so simple. For hundreds of years Serbs, Croats, Muslims, Montenegrins, Macedonians and Slovenes lived side by side often in mixed towns and villages. An alternative view is that the war came about because of politicians wishing to further their own ambitions. Whatever the causes, the wars of former Yugoslavia have resulted in hardship and misery for countless people. There is little wonder that the war has been called the 'Balkan tragedy'.

The Federal Parliament building in Belgrade, the capital of the former Yugoslavia.

End of an era

'Tito was the country's last unifying force; for many he was the glue that held Yugoslavia together until 1980... Tito's death in 1980 marked the end of an era. At the time no one could even have imagined the dramatic changes that were in store for Yugoslavia in the next decade.'
Carole Rogel, a modern day historian

Balkan background

The first people to inhabit the Balkans were tribes of hunters and gatherers during the 8th century BC. About 1200 BC the Albanians settled in the region and they were followed by large numbers of Southern Slavs who migrated from Asia between AD 500 and 700. The Southern Slavs settled in different parts of the Balkans and, over the centuries, they split into different groups, each with their own culture, traditions and sense of identity. The Slovenes and Croats settled in the northwest of the Balkans becoming Roman Catholics and using the Latin alphabet. The Serbs, Macedonians and Montenegrins settled in the east and south of the region, becoming Orthodox Christians and using the Greek or **Cyrillic alphabet**.

Two empires

During the 14th century the Islamic Turks swept through the Balkans. They routed the Serbs in the Battle of Kosovo Polje in 1389 and Serbia became part of the **Ottoman** (Turkish) **Empire**. By 1463 the Turks had also conquered Bosnia-Herzegovina, a country peopled by Croats and Serbs. After this many people in Bosnia converted from Christianity to Islam, in return for not having to pay taxes to the Turks. A separate Muslim culture grew up in Bosnia with its own architecture, customs and folklore.

An etching of the battle of Kosovo Polje, which took place between the Turks and the Serbs on 28 June 1389. Although the Serbs were defeated the battle became lodged in Serbian folklore.

Slovenia and Croatia had a different experience. By the early 1500s they had both been taken over by the **Habsburg Empire** and were **administered** from Vienna. The Balkans were now divided between two large rival empires. The Habsburgs set up a military frontier called the *vojna krajina* that ran along the southern border of Croatia. Here, soldiers were stationed to protect the Habsburg Empire from Turkish attacks.

In 1690 the Serbs revolted against their Turkish rulers. The rising was ruthlessly crushed. About 70,000 Serbs fled from the Turks. Some went to the *vojna krajina* to be employed as soldiers. In return they were excused taxes, given free land and allowed to practise the Orthodox religion. Other Serbs moved northwards from Kosovo into the fertile Habsburg-held Vojvodina. Albanians moved into Kosovo to inhabit the space left by the fleeing Serbs. In this way the various groups of Southern Slavs became intermingled. The distribution of ethnic settlement, however, did not correspond with the borders of countries and this was to spell trouble in later years.

Black George
Djordje Petrovic, nicknamed 'Karageorge' (Black George), a Serbian pig dealer and founder of the Karadjordjevic royal **dynasty**, led a revolt against the Turks in 1804. He was murdered in 1817 by Milos Obrenovic, the leader of a rival Serbian family. Karageorge's head was stuffed and sent to Istanbul!

The growth of nationalism

By the early 19th century the Turkish Empire was beginning to crumble. The peoples of the Balkans under Turkish rule began to press for independence. In 1830 Greece achieved its independence after an armed uprising. The following years saw an upsurge in Serbian **nationalism**. In 1844 Ilija Garasanin drew up a document called the *Outline* which said that all Serbs, wherever they lived in the Balkans, should be united into a Greater Serbia, free of Turkish rule. Ante Starcevic, the leader of the 'Party of Right' and a Croatian nationalist, called for Croatia to be independent of the **Habsburg Empire**.

In 1875 a Bulgarian revolt against Turkish rule was ruthlessly crushed. In one month alone 12,000 Christian Bulgarians were slaughtered by Turkish troops. Russia declared war on Turkey on the pretext of protecting Christians from the forces of Islam. The Congress of Vienna (1878) settled the dispute. The Congress stated that Bosnia-Herzegovina was to be **administered** by Austria-Hungary, and Bulgaria and Serbia were recognized as independent states.

The Eastern Question

The weakness of the Turkish Empire gave rise to the Eastern Question: What would happen to the Balkans if the Turks lost control of all their land? The great powers of Europe all had a view on this question:

- *Austria-Hungary* knew that if the Turkish Empire collapsed and broke up into independent countries, this would encourage people within its own empire to do the same. Austria-Hungary therefore looked to increase its influence in the Balkans.

- *Russia* wanted the Balkans to be free of the Turks. Like most of the people in the Balkans, the Russians were Slavs. Independent Balkan countries would be friendly towards Russia and allow it to have access to the Mediterranean Sea.

- *Britain* was anxious to uphold the Turkish Empire. If one power acquired more territory in the Balkans at the expense of another, it would upset the balance of power and make war more likely.

The Balkan Wars, 1912–13

In 1908 Austria-Hungary formally **annexed** Bosnia-Herzegovina. This infuriated Serbia who wanted to absorb the one million Bosnian Serbs into a Greater Serbia. The Serbs now looked southwards to expand their territory. In 1912 a new Turkish government tried to impose restrictive laws on Macedonia. This caused Greece, Serbia, Montenegro and Bulgaria to unite and form the Balkan League, which aimed to drive the Turks out of the Balkans once and for all. In the first Balkan War (1912) Turkey lost almost all of its territory in the Balkans. The Serbs captured Kosovo during the fighting. Serbia, Greece and Bulgaria then quarrelled over who should have Macedonia. In the second Balkan War of 1913, Bulgaria launched an attack on Serbia and Greece but was soon beaten. The Treaty of Bucharest (1913) divided Macedonia between Serbia and Greece. The Austrians were worried about the growing strength of Serbia and began looking for the chance to teach the Serbs a lesson. They did not have to wait long!

Serbian women receiving military training during the Balkan Wars of 1912–13.

The Pig War

Serbia's main source of income came from exporting pigs. Between 1906 and 1911 Austria-Hungary stopped buying pigs from Serbia. The Serbs opened up trade with Greece and, instead of losing money, increased their income! The 'Pig War' increased the distrust between Serbia and Austria-Hungary.

The birth of Yugoslavia

On 28 June 1914 Archduke Franz Ferdinand, the heir to the Austrian throne, paid a state visit to Sarajevo, the capital city of Bosnia. It was St Vitus' Day, the anniversary of the Battle of Kosovo Polje. While driving through the streets Franz Ferdinand and his pregnant wife, Sophie, were shot dead by Gavrilo Princip, a young Bosnian Serb student and member of the **Black Hand Society**. Austria believed that the assassination had been planned by the Serbian government and on 28 July 1914 Austria declared war on the Serbs. Within a week the great European powers had been sucked into the dispute and the First World War was underway.

The Serbian army on retreat in 1915 during the First World War.

The Kingdom of Serbs, Croats and Slovenes

The Austrians invaded Serbia and, by 1915, had forced the Serbian army to retreat into Albania and Greece. Here the Serbs retrained and they later fought their way back into Serbia. Meanwhile, in 1917 a South Slav Committee had been set up with the aim of establishing a South Slav state after the war. Some people had been calling for this to happen for almost a century.

On 3 November 1918 the Austrians surrendered and the **Habsburg Empire** was broken up. On 1 December 1918 Serbia (including Kosovo), Croatia, Bosnia, Slovenia, Montenegro and Macedonia were merged to form the Kingdom of Serbs, Croats and Slovenes. It was to be ruled by King Alexander I of Serbia.

What kind of a country?

Immediately there were arguments because power was divided unequally. The Serbs had more power in the parliament than the Croats and Slovenes. Many argued that the country should not be ruled directly from the centre. Instead it should have a **federal** structure with each region running its own affairs and the central government being responsible for just defence and foreign policy. There were fierce arguments and in 1928 Punisa Racic, a Montenegrin, shot five Croat deputies in parliament. In 1929 King Alexander suspended parliament and renamed the country Yugoslavia. He ruled on his own until 1931 in the hope of uniting the people. Although parliament was allowed to meet again in 1934, the arguing continued. The Croats still felt cheated and repeated the call for a federal style of government. Alexander I was sensationally assassinated on a visit to Marseilles, France, in 1934 and was succeeded by his brother, Prince Paul, who continued to rule without parliament. When the Second World War broke out in 1939 the future of Yugoslavia remained in the balance.

The assassination of King Alexander I

On 9 October 1934 Alexander I arrived in the French port of Marseilles. As his car was driving from the harbour, Vlada Gheorghieff, a Macedonian, opened fire with a Mauser pistol. The King was hit and he died on the floor of the car.

The French Foreign Minister, Louis Barthou, was also shot as he tried to protect the King. A soldier escorting the car lashed out at Gheorghieff with a sabre, only to wound the chauffeur instead. Finally, a policeman struck Gheorghieff a blow to the head and, as he fell, the crowd trampled on his body. He died later that evening from his injuries.

A French policeman strikes the assassin with a sword but it is too late to save Alexander I.

Enter Josip Broz Tito

On 6 April 1941 Nazi Germany invaded Yugoslavia. Using **blitzkrieg** tactics they quickly overran the country and the young King Peter II, who had replaced Prince Paul after a **coup** less than a month before, was forced into exile. The Germans and their Italian allies divided Yugoslavia into zones of occupation. Ante Pavelic, leader of the fascist **Ustasha** movement, was allowed to control an Independent State of Croatia, although it was really independent of the Nazis in name only. The Ustasha went on the rampage against minority groups within Croatia in what has been called **ethnic cleansing**. Thousands of Serbs, Jews and Gypsies were callously murdered. Orthodox Christian Serbs were ordered to become Roman Catholics. If they refused they were killed. The bloodshed was horrific and senseless.

Resistance groups

Two resistance groups, the Serbian **Chetniks** led by Draza Mihailovic and the **communist Partisans** led by Josip Broz Tito, emerged to fight the Germans. At first the groups fought together, but they soon fell out. The Chetniks wanted to bring the King back to rule Yugoslavia, while the Partisans wanted to make the country a socialist republic. The two groups began to fight each other as well as the Ustasha and the Germans. It was a war within a war.

A group of Tito's Partisans on the march in Belgrade in 1945.

The Partisans proved to be the dominant group. By 1943 Tito had a fighting force of 50,000 and he was strong enough to form a provisional government, even though Yugoslavia was still occupied. With British and Soviet help he gradually began to push the Germans out.

Brotherhood and Unity

In 1945 Tito set up the second Yugoslav state. It was a **communist** country run on a **federal** system. Tito wanted all the Southern Slavs to live in a country where there was 'brotherhood and unity' and ethnic hatred was a thing of the past. Tito's brand of communism allowed some private enterprise in the economy. This was particularly true of the tourist industry. The Adriatic coast became a popular foreign destination for thousands of holidaymakers. Tito also allowed consumer goods to be imported from abroad so that, in general, the Yugoslavs enjoyed a higher standard of living than other communist countries at the time.

While he was in power Tito held the country together. Schoolchildren learned about the history and culture of all the Slav groups. Yugoslavian national sporting teams drew on players from *all* of the republics and performed with pride and skill. Although people were not allowed to criticize the communist government, different ethnic groups were living side by side and in peace in the republics. There was, however, some bad feeling between the ethnic groups. For example, Slovenia and Croatia, the two richest republics resented having to pass some of their wealth on to the poorer southern parts of Yugoslavia. In 1971–2 Croatian nationalists carried out a campaign calling for Croatia to break away from Yugoslavia. Tito crushed the rising, imprisoned the leaders and the crisis faded away. But by the end of the 1970s, Tito's health was beginning to fail. What would happen to the country if he died?

The Socialist Federal Republic of Yugoslavia 1945–92

Head of Federal Government (Belgrade)
Controls defence, foreign policy and the federal army

Linked to six socialist republics

| Serbia (including provinces of Kosovo and Vojvodina) | Bosnia-Herzegovina | Croatia | Montenegro | Slovenia | Macedonia |

Each republic had its own parliament and ran its own local affairs – schools, hospitals etc.
Each republic sent representatives to sit in the Federal Parliament in Belgrade.

How the Socialist Federal Republic of Yugoslavia, set up by Tito, was organized between 1945 and 1992.

Turning point: the death of Tito

On 4 May 1980 Tito died at the age of 88. The majority of the Yugoslav people greeted his death with dismay. At his funeral people wept with grief. Tito had previously ordered that a collective presidency should run Yugoslavia after his death. This meant that a group of eight people, one from each republic and one each from the provinces of Vojvodina and Kosovo would be in control. The members took it in turns to chair the group on an annual basis.

> 'We all cried, but we did not know we were also burying Yugoslavia.'
> **Mahmut Bakali, an ethnic Albanian communist, on the occasion of Tito's funeral**

Economic problems

The collective presidency turned out to be a clumsy system. The eight members soon argued about how to deal with Yugoslavia's growing economic problems. Tito had borrowed large amounts of money to buy foreign consumer goods and to build factories. The country was having difficulty in paying this money back and by 1980 was US$19 billion dollars in debt. In addition, the price of everyday necessities was rising while wages remained at the same level. To try to solve the problem the government printed more money. This made things worse and by 1987 **inflation** was running at 200 per cent per year. People within Yugoslavia began to question and criticize the **communist** system. Workers went on strike calling for higher wages and lower prices.

Serb nationalism

In the 1980s the idea of creating a Greater Serbia was revived and there was an upsurge in Serb **nationalism**. This was illustrated by events in Kosovo, the poorest region of Yugoslavia, where 1.7 million Albanians and 200,000 Serbs lived. The Kosovo Albanians did not like being controlled by Serbia and began a series of attacks on the Serb minority. Crops were burned, people were assaulted, and there were allegations of rape and murder. The Kosovo Serbs called for protection from the Serbian government in Belgrade. In April 1987 the Serbian President, Ivan Stambolic, sent his friend Slobodan Milosevic to Kosovo to investigate the situation. Up to now Milosevic, the leader of the League of Communists of Serbia, had shown little interest in the problems of Kosovo Serbs. Large crowds of Serbs turned out to greet him in Kosovo Polje, on the outskirts of the capital city Pristina. Here Milosevic told the Serbs that, 'Yugoslavia and Serbia will not give up Kosovo.' Overnight, Milosevic became a hero and he realized he could use the growing spirit of nationalism to further his own political ambitions. With the support of the Yugoslav Federal Army (JNA) Milosevic ousted Stambolic from power and by 1989 had become the President of Serbia.

Milosevic used huge rallies and the press to promote his image and stir up Serb nationalism. He said he spoke for all Serbs, including those living in Croatia and Bosnia. On 28 March 1989 Kosovo had its **autonomous** rights removed and was brought under the direct rule of the Serbian government. Milosevic wanted Serbia to control the Yugoslav federation. The other republics were wary of him and they, too, began to assert their authority. There were problems ahead.

1988. Albanian nationalists in Pristina, Kosovo, demonstrate at the dismissal of their leaders. There was much Albanian ill-feeling towards the ruling Serb minority.

Discontent in Slovenia and Croatia

During 1989 **communist** governments collapsed in quick succession throughout Eastern Europe. In 1990, the League of Communists of Yugoslavia said that other parties could stand in elections. Given the demand for democracy in Europe they had no choice. Change was on the way.

Slovenia demands independence

Slovenia was disillusioned with being part of **Federal** Yugoslavia. Slovenia owned much of Yugoslavia's industry and had more wealth than the other republics. As a result it was made to pay the largest amount of money into the federal budget. Much of this money went to support the poorer parts of the country such as Kosovo. Many Slovenes also resented having to do compulsory military service in the Yugoslav Federal Army.

In 1989 the leader of the League of Communists of Slovenia, Milan Kucan, clashed with Milosevic. Slovenia expressed its support for the ethnic Albanians in Kosovo and Kucan called the Serbian leader 'an enemy of democracy'. A furious Milosevic declared a trade war on Slovenia and banned the import of Slovenian goods. The Slovenes enthusiastically supported Kucan's stand and were fully behind him as he called for independence.

Slovenia Factfile for 1991	
Population:	1,970,000
Area:	20,251 sq km
Capital:	Ljubljana
Ethnic groups:	Slovenes (87.8%)
	Hungarians (0.4%)
	Italians (0.2%)
	Others (11.6%)
Language:	Slovene
Exports:	US $4,810 million

Nationalism in Croatia

In Croatia, Franjo Tudjman, leader of the non-Communist Croatian Democratic Union, was elected President on 22 April 1990. Tudjman wanted Croatia to be independent, arguing that being part of a federal Yugoslavia was preventing economic progress. Tudjman's speeches were full of **nationalistic** rhetoric and remarks such as 'Thank God, my wife is not a Jew or a Serb'. His nationalistic fervour revived memories of the **Ustasha's** orgy of killing during the Second World War. For example, he took no action when the graves of Serbs killed by the Ustasha were vandalized by Croats, and he openly showed his contempt for the 600,000 Serbs living in Croatia.

Croatian nationalism spread beyond the borders of Croatia. Croats in Maastricht in the Netherlands march to show their support for the nationalist cause.

Under Tudjman, life was made difficult for the Croatian Serbs. Those employed by the government – teachers, police, judges and army personnel – were dismissed. The Latin alphabet, which was not used by Serbs, was declared the country's official alphabet. To get insurance and a driving licence people had to produce a form proving that they were of Croatian blood. To the Serbs the situation was intolerable and many left Croatia. In the Serbian areas of Croatia, however, Serbs turned on Croats, driving them from their homes and stealing their belongings. Where was all this unrest leading?

Croatia Factfile for 1991

Population:	4,688,507
Area:	56,538 sq km
Captial:	Zagreb
Ethnic groups:	Croats 78.1%
	Serbs 12.2 %
	Others 9.7%
Language:	Serbo-Croat
Exports:	US $3,300 million*

*This figure is an estimate based on available figures for nine months only

Turning point: Slovenia breaks away

In January 1990 the Congress of the League of **Communists** of Yugoslavia was called to discuss the future of the country. By this time Croatia and Slovenia had already allowed other political parties to be formed and elections were planned for the spring. Milosevic of Serbia wanted Yugoslavia to be kept intact as a federation. Kucan, however, was adamant that Slovenia wanted to break away and have its independence. Milosevic refused to accept this and the Slovene delegation walked out of the Congress, heralding the disintegration of the **federal** Communist Party and the inevitable break up of Yugoslavia.

Towards the end of 1990 further talks were held to see if an agreement could be made about forming a new Yugoslavia now that one-party Communist rule had collapsed. The Slovenes and Serbs refused to shift from their positions. In December a referendum was held in Slovenia and the people voted overwhelmingly for independence. Slovenia and Croatia then announced that they intended to break away from Yugoslavia.

The Federal President of Yugoslavia, Ante Markovic, was horrified and called for the two republics to change their minds. He travelled to Zagreb to address the Croatian parliament only to be howled down. The noise was so loud that it took some time for the Speaker to restore order. On 25 June 1991 Croatia and Slovenia declared their independence.

The Ten Days War

The Slovenian border guards took immediate action. They removed the signs 'Yugoslavia' from the border posts with Austria, Hungary and Italy and replaced them with signs saying 'Slovenia'. They also placed border posts along the frontier with Croatia. Units of the Serb-dominated Yugoslav Federal Army (JNA) were now sent into action. Tanks appeared on the streets of Ljubljana, the capital city, and JNA troops attacked the border posts set up by the Slovenians. The Slovenians were prepared for the fight and fought back bravely. Before the declaration of independence the Slovenian Defence Minister, Janez Jansa, had bought enough arms to take on the JNA in a short war. On 27 June a helicopter taking supplies to the JNA was shot down over Ljubljana, killing the pilot and mechanic on board.

It's war!

'I realized that this was not a revolt or political demonstration, but that it was war. We realized that the Slovenes wanted to kill us, to shoot us, that there was no Yugoslavia and that there was no more life together with them.'
General Milan Aksentijevic of the Yugoslav Federal Army

Lorries burn in Slovenia as the country descends into a brutal war.

Truce

After ten days of fighting the war came to an end when a truce was negotiated by the **European Community (EC)**. The world sympathized with the Slovenians and condemned the federal government of Yugoslavia. Douglas Hurd, the British Foreign Minister, said 'The time has passed when you could keep a state together by shooting its citizens'. Milosevic came to accept the fact that Slovenia had broken away; unlike other Yugoslav republics it did not have a large Serb minority within its borders. In January 1992 Slovenia was recognized as an independent country by the EC and in May 1992 it was admitted into the **United Nations**.

Turning point: War in Croatia

The First Serb-Croat War 1991

The mixed peoples of Croatia had lived in peace together during the rule of Tito. Despite their differences in religion and culture most Croats and Serbs mixed well together.

The reawakening of Croat **nationalism** by President Tudjman produced a different atmosphere. Peace-loving Croatians from each of the ethnic groups feared for the future. After Croatia declared independence from **Federal** Yugoslavia on 25 June 1991 the country descended into a bitter civil war. Many Serbs in Croatia thought that Tudjman intended to wipe out their culture and way of living and prepared to fight.

Both the Serbs and the Croats formed militia groups, made up of armed extremists. The Croatian Serbs set up **Chetnik** militia groups named after the Second World War resistance fighters. These groups wanted to join with Serbia and be ruled by a monarch again. They carried a black flag that had a white skull and crossbones with the words 'Freedom or death' underneath. The Croats formed **Ustasha** groups. They modelled themselves on the Ustasha of the 1940s, wearing black uniforms and using the Nazi salute.

The official army of Croatia, the National Guard, was poorly equipped and organized and could do little against the powerful Serb militias that were supplied with arms by Milosevic. The Croatian National Guard had to commandeer vans and buses for transport, but the Serb militias had armoured cars. Just as in Slovenia, the Serb-dominated Yugoslav Federal Army (JNA) moved in, supposedly to keep the two factions apart. In practice there were numerous instances where the JNA sided with the Serb militias.

The events in Osijek and Kijevo serve to show the level of senseless violence that became common in Croatia in 1991. In Osijek, the Croat police blew up a house that they said was a base for Serb terrorists. When they inspected the ruins all they found were the bodies of an innocent man and his mother. Kijevo was a Croat village situated in Serb territory. Ante Martic, the leader of a Serb militia called the Marticevci, decided to wipe it off the map. With the help of the JNA, Martic flattened the village in a twelve-hour long bombardment. Afterwards he boasted that the village had been 'cleansed' of Croats and that he 'didn't care about the victims.' Unsurprisingly other Croats in Serbian-held areas fled before they became victims of the violence. Often they left all their possessions behind in their anxiety to get to safety.

Fighting between Serbs and Croats in the university town of Osijek, north-eastern Croatia, July 1991.

Serbs and Croats together

In the mixed village of Miokovicevo Croats and Serbs together fought off an attack by a Croatian militia group. The villagers decided to go to Bosnia for safety. On the way they were stopped by Serbian soldiers who stole their money and possessions. When they reached Bosnia the authorities separated the Croats in the group from the Serbs. The Croats were never seen again. One Serb villager said: 'I only know for sure that they didn't dare return to Croatia because they would have been shot for fighting for their village on our side.'

The destruction of Vukovar

On 26 August 1991 Vukovar, a town in north-eastern Croatia near the frontier with Serbia, came under fierce attack from the combined forces of the JNA and Serb militia groups. Vukovar, on the banks of the river Danube, had a population of 84,000, 44 per cent of whom were Croat and 37 per cent Serb. Before the war the mixed population lived together peacefully. Many of the town's Serbs were against the war and refused to leave their homes when the town came under attack. The Serbs and JNA were anxious to capture the town because it would put them in control of a region that had oil and rich farming land.

Siege

The town was put under siege. The attackers brought in tanks, armoured cars and heavy artillery and bombarded the town daily with over 5000 shells. Croat militia groups were left to defend the town without help from the Croatian government. Some Croats accused President Tudjman of sacrificing the town for propaganda purposes. They said he wanted to show the Serbs as the aggressors so that Croatia would get the sympathy of western powers such as the USA and Britain.

The bombardment, including bombing raids, was so fierce that people were forced to leave their homes and go into communal basement shelters where they stayed for the duration of the siege. A crisis committee was formed to ensure people had food and water. Patients in the hospital were moved to the basement where they were treated.

Tudjman reacts angrily

The military commander in charge of defending Vukovar, Mile Dedakovic, visited President Tudjman in Zagreb to ask for weapons and armaments. Tudjman was reluctant to get involved. He wanted to sort things out by negotiation and angrily reminded Dedakovic that he was the President of Croatia and running the war was his responsibility.

Rubble

On 18 November 1991 the Croat defenders surrendered and the siege came to an end. The whole of the town except the hospital was in Serb hands. When the townspeople came out of their shelters they could not believe their eyes. The town had been reduced to a heap of rubble. Even worse was to follow. Croat soldiers were taken away in trucks and executed. In 1992 a mass grave was found outside the town with the bodies of hundreds of people. Croat civilians were forced to leave Vukovar and go to other parts of Croatia. Afterwards Serbs who themselves had been made homeless by Croats moved into the town from other areas of eastern Croatia. Following the siege little was done to rebuild the town.

The Croats made Vukovar a symbol of Croatian heroism in the face of Serb aggression, but it was not until 1997 that the Serbs withdrew from the town.

Aftermath of the siege
89% of housing destroyed
(of which 68% completely);
1851 soldiers killed;
2464 wounded;
Over 3000 civilians killed;
Thousands described as 'missing';
80,000 Croats from Vukovar and
the surrounding villages forced to
leave for other parts of Croatia as
displaced persons.

Serb militiamen make their way through the ruins of Vukovar, November 1991.

Dubrovnik bombarded

Dubrovnik, a medieval walled city, in the southernmost part of Croatia was attacked from Montenegro by the Serb-dominated JNA on 1 October 1991. During the rule of Tito, Dubrovnik and the nearby coastal holiday resorts had attracted millions of holidaymakers from abroad. The city itself had many historical buildings and was a world heritage site. It was known as the 'pearl of the Adriatic'.

Reasons for the attack

Dubrovnik had a predominantly Croat population of 50,000. Only 6000 Serbs lived in the city. Before the war there had been no friction between the Serbs and their Croat neighbours and there was no military garrison. Publicly, the JNA said that the Croats were harassing the Serbs of Dubrovnik, but in reality their motives were very different. If the JNA captured Dubrovnik and its port, Gruz, Serbia would have access to the sea via Bosnia. In addition, the Serbs believed that capturing this beautiful city would provide them with a powerful bargaining tool in any peace talks that were to arise.

Dubrovnik, the 'pearl of the Adriatic', under attack by the Serb-dominated Yugoslav Federal Army (JNA), October 1991.

Dubrovnik was shelled from the sea and land. Many old buildings were damaged but the ancient city walls, up to six metres thick in places, stood up well to the battering. People inside the city retreated into cramped shelters that lacked electricity and fresh water. The shelling went on for days. Boats in the harbour were blown up in what appeared to be gratuitous violence. The Croat towns and villages on the outskirts of Dubrovnik were looted and burnt as people fled from the JNA and Montenegrin militiamen.

The shelling of Dubrovnik shocked the world. The event was widely publicized on television and in the press and public opinion sided with the Croats. What was not so widely reported, however, were the Croat attacks on Serbian towns and villages such as Sisak and Gospic. Hundreds of Serbs were killed and their houses torched. About 500,000 Serbs fled their homes to escape the violence. But by December the Serbs had captured one-third of Croatia. They called the areas captured *Republika Srpska Krajina* (Serb Republic of Krajina).

A propaganda stunt: the Happy Convoy

On 30 October 1991 Stipe Mesic, the Croat representative in the **Federal** Yugoslav Collective Presidency, assembled a convoy of small pleasure boats with the aim of breaking the JNA's naval blockade of Dubrovnik. On board were several famous Croats, such as Tereza Kesovija, a popular singer. Outside Dubrovnik harbour, Mesic told the JNA commander to let them through. The commander replied that if the convoy went any further he would open fire. Eventually, after the convoy was searched for arms it was allowed into the harbour. The escapade successfully publicized the plight of Dubrovnik.

Attempts at peace

In September 1991 Macedonia declared itself independent. Federal Yugoslavia was falling apart. In the same month the **European Community (EC)** set up a peace conference in The Hague, under the chairmanship of Lord Carrington. Over the next two months the EC negotiated thirteen ceasefires between the Serbs and Croats, all of which were broken! On 23 November Cyrus Vance, working on behalf of the **United Nations** (UN), negotiated a ceasefire to come into effect on 2 January 1992.

The Second Serb-Croat War 1995

Although Croatia was now independent, the country was divided. One third of Croatia was under Serb control. On 21 February 1992 a **United Nations (UN)** Protection Force (UNPROFOR) moved into those parts of Croatia held by the Serbs which they had named the independent Serb Republic of the Krajina. Four protection areas were established as the UN sought to bring peace and stability. The UN's task was to demilitarize the protected areas and prepare the ground for the eventual withdrawal of the JNA. In addition it would protect the local Serb population and help displaced people to get back to their homes. It was a tall order!

The troubles continue

The Croats wanted the Krajina back under their control. They mounted a campaign to drive the Serbs out. In 1993 Croat forces attacked a group of Serb villages around Medak forcing the people to leave their homes. They then burnt the houses, killed all the livestock and poisoned the wells. A UN report said that the area had been turned into a wasteland. Neither side was prepared to give up their weapons and the Serbs refused point blank to negotiate a solution about the future of the Krajina. In 1994 Slobodan Milosevic told the Serbs in Croatia that he could no longer support them and they were on their own.

War again

By 1995 the Croatian army had reorganized and was much better equipped than it had been in 1991. On 1 May 1995 it launched 'Operation Flash', a surprise attack on Serb-held territory around Pakrac in the Krajina. The Croats said they went on the offensive because the Serb militia groups kept blockading the main highway in the region. The following day the Serbs fired shells on Zagreb killing 6 people and wounding 175. The UN was powerless to stop the fighting.

An injured victim of the Serb shelling of Zagreb waiting to be transported to hospital, 2 May 1995.

On 4 August 1995 the Croats, helped by Bosnian Muslims, launched 'Operation Storm'. About 150,000 troops were sent into action and within five days they recaptured most of the territory seized by the Serbs in 1991. The major Serb towns of Knin and Glina were both captured. Serb troops fled the area leaving the civilians to look after themselves. There was an exodus of 200,000 Serbs who fled over the border into Bosnia and Serbia. As they did so the Croats shelled them. Many Serbs who stayed in their villages, usually the old and infirm, were shot. Several villages were burnt to the ground. The UN reported that it had inspected 389 Serb villages and had found that 17,000 houses out of 22,000 had been destroyed or badly damaged.

'Croats launch huge attack to recapture rebel region'

'Croatia launched a huge co-ordinated attack involving aircraft, armour and artillery along a 400-mile front in the Krajina region yesterday to recapture territory from the rebel Serbs, plunging the country into depths of violence not seen since the beginning of the conflict. Early reports said that Croat troops had made significant gains in the north of the region that was lost to the Serbs in 1991.'
Daily Telegraph – 5 August 1995

Serb civilians fleeing from Knin, in southern Croatia, ahead of the attack by Croat forces, August 1995.

The road to war in Bosnia

Factfile – Bosnia in 1991

Population:	4,422,000
Area:	51,129 sq km
Capital:	Sarajevo
Ethnic groups:	Muslims: 44%
	Serbs: 31%
	Croats: 17%
Language:	Serbo-Croat, Bosnian
Exports:	US $2,187 million

Apart from a period during the Second World War, Muslims, Serbs and Croats in Bosnia had lived peacefully together for centuries. Few settlements across the republic were ethnically **homogenous**. There had also been intermarrying and such people preferred to call themselves 'Yugoslavs'. By April 1992, however, Bosnia had become the scene of a tragic war.

Multiparty elections

On 9 November 1990 the first multiparty elections were held in Bosnia. About 75 per cent of those who voted did so for one of the **nationalist** parties (see box). Afterwards all three parties governed the country in a partnership under the leadership of the Muslim President, Alija Izetbegovic. During 1991, however, the wars in Slovenia and Croatia served to destabilize Bosnia and arguments between the three ethnic groups developed.

The burning question was: what should Bosnia do if Slovenia and Croatia were successful in breaking away from **Federal** Yugoslavia? Radovan Karadzic, the leader of the Bosnian Serbs, was adamant that Bosnia should remain part of Yugoslavia. The Muslims and Croats argued that this would leave them in a Yugoslavia dominated by Serbs and that it would be better to be independent. President Izetbegovic said it was like having a choice between 'leukaemia and a brain tumour'. Whichever course Bosnia took would result in trouble.

Political Parties formed in Bosnia in 1990

Name of Party	Ethnic Group	Leader
Party of Democratic Action (SDA)	Muslims	Alija Izetbegovic
Serbian Democratic Party (SDS)	Serbs	Radovan Karadzic
Croatian Democratic Union in Bosnia (HDZ)	Croats	Franjo Boras

Propaganda

Karadzic began to be obstructive in parliament, arguing that if Bosnia became independent 'it would bring a hell in which the Muslims would perish'. Propaganda stories were spread in the press alleging that the Muslims wanted to take over Bosnia and convert everyone to the Islamic faith. If they refused, the stories went, they would be killed. The stories were untrue but many non-Muslims believed them. Weapons were transported into Bosnia from Serbia and gradually the Bosnian Serbs built up an army. In November 1991 the Bosnian Serbs held a referendum among themselves and a large majority said they wanted to remain as part of Yugoslavia. Following this they proclaimed the formation of an **autonomous** Serb 'republic' within Bosnia that had its own government and currency. It was named the *Republika Srpska*. Karadzic was in constant touch with Slobodan Milosevic and he also knew he had the support of the JNA.

President Izetbegovic was terrified of a war in Bosnia and felt that the best way forward was to have an independent Bosnia in which the ethnic groups shared power. He was encouraged by a large peace demonstration that took place in Sarajevo in November 1991. Thousands took to the streets carrying photographs of Tito and 'Brotherhood and Unity' banners. But their hopes were soon to be dashed.

A panoramic view of Sarajevo, the capital city of Bosnia, taken in 1984. Seven years later it was to be the scene of fierce fighting.

Bosnia's referendum

On 15 January 1992 the **European Community (EC)** announced that it was recognizing the independence of Slovenia and Croatia. It was a controversial decision. The German Chancellor, Helmut Kohl, had campaigned hard for the EC to come to this decision. Lord Carrington, the EC's peace envoy to Yugoslavia and former British foreign secretary, was nervous about the decision and expressed his doubts publicly.

In February 1992 the EC held a conference in Lisbon, Portugal, to see if an agreement could be reached on the future of Bosnia. The outcome was a plan to divide Bosnia up into three separate parts based on ethnic groupings. This would be difficult to achieve as the three groups were not altogether each in their own area. The only way to make it work was to move people from area to area. Izetbegovic initially agreed to the plan but then changed his mind, as he felt it was unworkable.

Lord Carrington's view

'I said if they (the countries of the EC) recognized Croatia and Slovenia then they would have to ask all the others whether they wanted their independence. And if they asked the Bosnians they would say "yes" and this would mean a civil war in Bosnia.'

The EC had already suggested that Bosnia should hold a referendum to see if its people wanted independence. It was duly held between 28 February and 1 March. The Serbs were told to boycott the referendum so just the Croats and Muslims voted (61 per cent of the population). Of those who voted, 99 per cent said they wanted Bosnia to be independent.

Fighting erupts in Bosnia

Even before the results of the referendum had been announced there was trouble in Sarajevo. An unidentified masked gunman shot a Serb guest at a wedding, after which the Serb militia group, 'The **Tigers**', carried out a number of killings. On 2 April 1992 the same group raided the small town of Bijeljina on the Serbian border and murdered innocent Muslims. Many Bosnians knew the country was on the verge of all-out war and on 5 April, over 7000 people from all the ethnic groups walked through the streets of Sarajevo calling for a multi-ethnic Bosnia.

Serb artilleries, positioned in the surrounding hills, bombard Sarajevo, May 1992.

Serb snipers opened fire on the marchers. Panic set in as the marchers ran for safety. In the evening the city was shelled by Serb guns located in the surrounding hills. The siege of Sarajevo had started. It lasted until 29 February 1996.

Independence

On 6 April 1992 Bosnia was recognized as an independent country by the EC and the USA. This was unacceptable to the Serbs. It appeared that the Croats and Muslims were being favoured and Karadzic said that the outside world had ignored the desires of the Serbs in Bosnia. The country was now plunged into war. Lord Carrington flew to Sarajevo to try to negotiate a ceasefire but it was too late.

The Federal Republic of Yugoslavia

On 27 April 1992 a new **Federal** Republic of Yugoslavia was declared, consisting of just Serbia (and its provinces of Kosovo and Vojvodina) and Montenegro. It had a population of 11 million. Its president was Dobrica Cosic.

Turning point: War in Bosnia

The United Nations acts

On 30 May 1992 the **United Nations** imposed economic sanctions on Serbia as a punishment for supporting the Bosnian Serbs. An embargo was placed on all trade, and oil supplies to Serbia were cut off. No commercial flights were allowed in and Serbia's overseas assets were frozen. The JNA was ordered to pull its soldiers out of Bosnia, but the heavily armed Bosnian Serb Army was left, under General Ratko Mladic, to continue the war. In June, 1000 UN soldiers were despatched to the besieged city of Sarajevo as part of UNPROFOR II. Their task was to protect the airport so that supplies could come in by air and to provide escorts for convoys of lorries bringing in food and medicine overland. This usually involved negotiating with Serb militiamen to remove road blocks they had built. However, there was nothing the UN could do to stop the Serbs gaining control of two-thirds of Bosnia by August.

During the first weeks of the war Serb militia groups carried out **blitzkrieg** style attacks on the predominantly Muslim areas of eastern and north-western Bosnia. Muslims were forced to flee from their villages and seek refuge in the towns of Srebrenica,

UN troops supervise emergency aid supplies for the besieged civilians of Sarajevo.

Tuzla and Bihac. The Bosnian Serbs wanted to control these areas and later to merge them with Serbia. In forcing Muslims out of the area the Serbs carried out terrible acts of violence: innocent civilians were murdered, tortured and raped.

Ethnic cleansing

'A Serb neighbour broke into my house one morning. He shot at our window. He then broke down the door, entered and started shelling the furniture. Then he barged into our room. The two of us, mother and I, with my little one, opened the window trying to jump out. Another man, waiting in the street, shot at me and the baby. I was lightly wounded. My little one, she was killed. Mother remained in the window. She was hit by the one in the street. They were yelling at us to get out, that they were cleansing the place. Yes, that's what they said.'
Sonja Piric, a Muslim refugee, from a village near Srebrenica

The Muslim and Croat minorities in Banja Luka, the capital of the Serb-proclaimed *Republika Srpska*, were terrorized into leaving the city. Their shops and restaurants were bombed, their cars taken and their homes attacked. Three mosques were destroyed and the rubble carted away. The Serbs were intent on ridding the city of all traces of Islamic culture. During the war as a whole, the Serbs were accused of committing more atrocities than anyone else. But it should be remembered that the Muslims and Croats also carried out their share of **ethnic cleansing** using similar tactics to the Serbs.

Loyal neighbours

Some Bosnian Serbs did not agree with the war and tried to help their Croat and Muslim neighbours. In Prijedor, in north-western Bosnia, four Muslim families were saved by a Serb who drove them to his father's farm in the countryside. Here they hid from the militiamen. Later the Serb was forced to join the Bosnian Serb Army. If he had refused his family would have been shot.

Detention camps exposed

During 1992 rumours began to circulate that Muslims and Croats were being held in detention camps run by the Bosnian Serbs. On 5 August the Serbs allowed American and British journalists to visit two camps at Omarska and Trnopolje. They were shocked at what they saw. The camps contained Muslim and Croat civilians who had either fled from their villages or been forced into the camps by the Serbs as part of **ethnic cleansing**. Photographs of skeletal, emaciated victims were splashed across the world's press and the Serbs were severely condemned. Atrocities beyond comprehension were committed in these camps, including rape and systematic killing. Men were forced to load corpses on to trucks, which took them to mass graves. People compared the camps to the extermination camps run by the Nazis during the Second World War. The more literate people, such as teachers and lecturers, were picked out for killing. If the best brains of the Croats and Muslims were wiped out they would not have anyone to lead them in the future.

The Vance-Owen Plan

In January 1993 Cyrus Vance, the UN peace envoy and Lord David Owen of the **European Union** published a plan which they hoped would end the fighting. They proposed that Bosnia should be divided into ten provinces or cantons according to ethnic groupings. There would be three cantons each for the Serbs, Croats and Muslims. In Sarajevo power was to be shared between the three groups. The Croats and Muslims accepted the plan. The Serbs, however, rejected the plan as it would mean giving up much of the territory they had captured in 1992.

Emaciated Bosnian Muslims, just after release from detention in a Croat prison.

The war escalates

In April 1993 the Croats and Muslims began fighting each other over the land that was not controlled by the Serbs. The Croats began to shell the divided city of Mostar. The western part of the city was Croatian and the eastern part was Muslim. The river Neretva, spanned by the Stari Most (Old Bridge) was the dividing line. The Croats aimed to drive the Muslims out of the city. In November 1993 the Old Bridge, built by the Turks when Bosnia was part of the **Ottoman Empire**, was blown up by the Croats. A detention centre was established where Muslims were imprisoned in huge fuel tanks. Many died from the fumes, while others were needlessly murdered by their Croat guards.

The Stari Most (Old Bridge) in Mostar, destroyed by the Croats in November 1993.

Cyrus Vance

Cyrus Vance was born in the USA in 1917. He started out in life as a lawyer and did not get involved in politics until 1961. He acquired a reputation as a skilful negotiator and diplomat, taking part in the Paris peace talks on Vietnam in 1968–9. Vance was appointed to be the UN's envoy in former Yugoslavia where, with David Owen, he worked tirelessly to bring a solution to the war in Bosnia.

Safe areas

Since 1992 Srebrenica, a Muslim town in eastern Bosnia, had been under siege by the Serbs. It had become a Muslim enclave in Serb-held territory and was in danger of being overrun by the Serbs. In April the town was made a UN 'safe area' in an effort to protect the Muslim inhabitants. A few weeks later Sarajevo, Goradze, Zepa, Tuzla and Bihac were also designated as safe areas. The UN secretary-general, Boutros Boutros-Ghali, asked for 35,000 troops to be sent to guard the towns. In the event the United Nations only managed to supply about 8000 soldiers which was insufficient to guarantee the protection of the safe areas from Serb attacks. On 5 February 1994 a mortar bomb, thought to have been fired by the Serbs, landed on the packed market place in the centre of Sarajevo killing 68 people and injuring almost 200. It was an event that triggered worldwide outrage and condemnation.

A victim of the mortar bomb fired on Sarajevo market place being pulled away from the scene, 5 February 1994.

Peace between Croats and Muslims

Behind the scenes there had been intense diplomatic activity by the USA to negotiate an agreement between the Croats and the Muslims. On 18 March 1994 the discussions came to fruition when President Tudjman of Croatia and President Izetbegovic of Bosnia signed the Washington Accords in the White House. They agreed to set up a Muslim-Croat Federation in Bosnia in which power would be shared between the two groups. It was a welcome step forward.

Bosnian Muslim refugees after they had been forced to leave Srebrenica by Bosnian Serbs, July 1995.

War against the Serbs continues

By now the Serbs were beginning to show signs of weakening. Oil was in short supply and the troops were losing heart. Men were refusing to enlist, causing a lack of manpower. The Muslims, however, had grown in strength and began to force the Serbs out of some of the areas they had taken at the start of the war. In December 1994 former American president, Jimmy Carter, helped to negotiate a ceasefire that lasted for four months.

In the summer of 1995 the Serbs made one last ditch attempt to consolidate their position in eastern Bosnia. On 11 July General Ratko Mladic advanced on Srebrenica with the intention of forcing the Muslims out. About 40,000 Muslim women, children and old people fled and a further 8000 men were reported to have been massacred in cold blood. There was nothing the 400 Dutch UN peacekeepers could do to stop the Serbs.

General Ratko Mladic

Mladic was born in 1943, the son of a **Partisan** resistance fighter. In April 1992 he was made the military commander of the Bosnian Serb Army and he planned the **blitzkrieg** attack on eastern Bosnia that resulted in the Serbs taking large amounts of territory. Mladic gained a reputation for his brutal tactics during the war. In 1994 his soldiers carried out a campaign against UNPROFOR, capturing hundreds of UN troops. He is wanted by the **War Crimes Tribunal** for his part in the killing of Bosnian Muslims in Srebrenica in 1995, but is still at large.

The tide turns

On 28 August 1995 a shell landed in Sarajevo market place once again, this time killing 35 people. **NATO** forces in Bosnia responded quickly and launched air strikes against Serb positions to the east and south of the city. Over twenty military targets were bombed including missile sites, ammunition depots and artillery emplacements. The air strikes continued for three weeks. In September the Serbs lost territory in fighting near Bihac and 50,000 Serb civilians fled the area on tractors and horse-drawn carts. Next, the Muslims won back land in central and southern Bosnia. Thousands of Serb civilians fled to Banja Luka seeking refuge. Their abandoned houses were looted and razed to the ground by the advancing Muslims. On 20 September the Serbs removed their heavy guns from around Sarajevo and allowed supplies into the city. The Serbs were exhausted and knew that the time had come to negotiate an end to the war.

The Dayton Peace Accord

On 11 October a 60-day ceasefire began, pending peace talks that were to be held at the Wright-Patterson Air Force base in Dayton, Ohio. The talks were the result of months of hard work behind the scenes by Richard Holbrooke, the USA's Balkan envoy. Over a three-week period Tudjman, Izetbegovic and Milosevic thrashed out an agreement. As an **indicted war criminal**, Karadzic was not allowed to take part in the discussions. By negotiating for the Bosnian Serbs and behaving in a moderate manner, Milosevic hoped that sanctions on Serbia, which was being strangled by the trade embargoes, would be lifted. The Dayton Peace Accord, formally signed on 14 December 1995, created the Union of Bosnia-Herzegovina that was to be divided into two separate self-governing republics: the Muslim-Croat Federation (51 per cent of the land) and Serb *Republika Srpska* (49 per cent of the land). Sarajevo was to be a multi-ethnic city under Muslim control.

The formal signing of the Dayton Peace Accord in Paris, 14 December 1995.
Left to right: Milosevic (Serbia), Izetbegovic (Bosnia) and Tudjman (Croatia).

The Union's presidency was to rotate between the Croats, Serbs and Muslims. The agreement also said that displaced people were to be allowed to return to their homes and that war criminals were to be tried. A NATO force of 60,000 men was to be sent to Bosnia to supervise the peace. The agreement was far from perfect and it was not long before political commentators were asking if the peace would last. The war in Bosnia had claimed the lives of 200,000 people and forced two million to leave their homes.

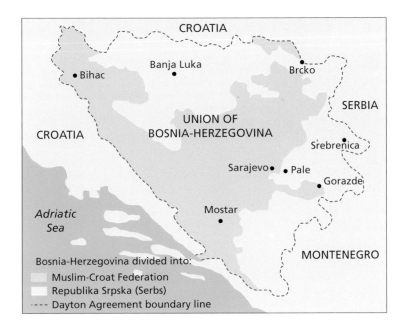

How Bosnia-Herzegovina was divided by the Dayton Peace Accord.

What they said about the Dayton Peace Accord

'In a civil war there are no winners and there could be no winner. All are losers. Only peace is a victory. The solutions achieved here include painful concessions by all sides.'
President Slobodan Milosevic of Serbia

'This may not be a just peace, but it is more just than a continuation of war.'
President Alija Izetbegovic of Bosnia

'The agreement will result in lasting peace and create conditions for the establishment of a new world order in this part of the world.'
President Franjo Tudjman of Croatia

Turning point: Conflict in Kosovo

During the 1990s Kosovo, a province of Serbia in the southern Balkans, was the scene of serious clashes between ethnic Albanians and Serbs that

Kosovo Factfile for 1991

Population:	1,900,000
Area:	10,897 sq km
Capital:	Pristina
Ethnic groups:	Albanians: 1,700,000 (90%)
	Serbs: 200,000 (10%)

culminated in a **NATO** bombing campaign in 1999. What was the background to this bitter conflict?

Albanians and Serbs

In the Middle Ages Kosovo was part of the ancient Kingdom of Serbia. On 28 June 1389 the invading Turks beat the Serbian leader, Prince Lazar, at the Battle of Kosovo Polje. Serbia and Kosovo became part of the **Ottoman Empire** for the next 500 years. During this time some Serbs left Kosovo and moved northwards to escape Turkish rule. They were replaced by Albanians who were attracted by the more fertile land. The Serbs, however, have always claimed Kosovo to be 'the cradle of their civilization' and the Battle of Kosovo Polje is an important symbol in Serbian culture.

The modern era

In the 19th century the Ottoman Empire fell into decay and in 1878 Serbia regained its independence, although Kosovo remained under Turkish rule. Following the first Balkan War of 1912, Serbian troops occupied Kosovo and, in 1918, it was incorporated into the Kingdom of Serbs, Croats and Slovenes. During the 1920s and 1930s the Albanian language was banned in Kosovo and thousands of Albanians were forced out of the region by the Serbs. In 1941 Kosovo was occupied by invading Italian forces who drove out an estimated 75,000 Serbs.

When Tito came to power in 1945, Kosovo was reincorporated into Yugoslavia and the ethnic Albanians were allowed to speak their own language. When, in 1968, groups of Albanians called for Kosovo to be joined to Albania, Tito had the ringleaders arrested and imprisoned. Six years later Kosovo was given full **autonomy** as a province within Serbia. Discontent, however, was brewing among the Albanians. Tito's death in 1980 brought further instability. In 1981 there were riots when Albanians demanded that Kosovo should become a separate republic. The Yugoslav government sent tanks into the region to quell the rioters. Throughout the 1980s Serbs claimed that their Albanian neighbours were making life intolerable.

'Exodus of Serbs stirs province in Yugoslavia'

'Serbs have reportedly been harassed by Albanians and have packed up and left the region. There were reports of Serbian farmers being pressured to sell their land cheap and of Albanian shopkeepers refusing to sell goods to Serbs. "We don't want to go because we have a large farm," a Serbian farmer's wife said in a village near Pristina. "Our property has not been touched, but there are the insults and the intimidation, so we feel uncomfortable."'
New York Times – 12 July 1982

On 28 March 1989, the Serbian President, Slobodan Milosevic took Kosovo's autonomy away and put the province under the direct rule of Belgrade. Then, three months later on the 600th anniversary of the Battle of Kosovo Polje, Milosevic addressed a rally of a million Serbs at Gazimestan. Appearing to stir up **nationalist** feeling he told the crowd 'Six centuries later again we are in battles and quarrels. They are not armed battles, though such things should not be excluded yet.' His words turned out to be prophetic.

Slobodan Milosevic addressing a crowd of one million Serbs on the 600th anniversary of the Battle of Kosovo Polje, 28 June 1989.

43

Descent into civil war

After 1989 the Serbs ran Kosovo directly and imposed a strict regime on the ethnic Albanians who were denied many human rights. Albanian students were banned from studying at Pristina University, Albanian workers were dismissed from their jobs and broadcasting in the Albanian language was banned. After violent street protests in February 1990 Serbia sent troops and tanks into Kosovo and imposed a curfew. The Albanians responded by declaring independence and setting up their own arrangements for education, health provision and taxation. The Albanian leader, Ibrahim Rugova, tried to negotiate a new **autonomy** agreement with Milosevic but without success.

The Kosovo Liberation Army

Militant Albanians grew impatient with the lack of progress and in 1997 the Kosovo Liberation Army (KLA) was formed. The KLA wanted Kosovo to be independent. KLA **guerrillas** carried out a series of hit and run ambushes on Serbian patrols and attacked police stations.

The Serbs took their revenge by attacking civilians, forcing thousands of Albanians out of their villages and torching their houses. The KLA then began to take control of towns and villages, which provoked the Serbs to launch a big attack in September 1998. Some 2000 Kosovo Albanians were killed and 250,000 fled from their homes over the border into Albania and Macedonia. The situation was getting out of control. Richard Holbrooke of the USA went to Belgrade and told Milosevic that **NATO** planes would bomb Serbia unless he ordered his troops

Kosovo Liberation Army recruits, 1999.

back to their barracks and agreed to a ceasefire. Milosevic agreed and a team of 2000 international observers, the Kosovo Verification Commission (KVC), went into Kosovo to supervise the truce. As the Serbs withdrew, the KLA moved into the space and took control of much of the province. An angry Milosevic sent Serbian troops back in and the fighting restarted. A series of tit-for-tat ethnic killings followed as Kosovo fell into anarchy.

The Rambouillet peace talks

On 15 January 1999, 45 Albanians were massacred in the village of Recak. NATO reacted by warning Milosevic that air strikes on Serbia would go ahead unless he ordered an end to the **ethnic cleansing**. Western leaders summoned Milosevic and the KLA to final talks at Rambouillet Château near Paris. The talks dragged on for three weeks before the KLA agreed to a peace plan to end the fighting. Kosovo would get self-rule back and an international

Albanians from the village of Recak in Kosovo burying the dead after the Serb attack on 15 January 1998.

peacekeeping force would be sent to the province. Milosevic, however, refused to accept such a force in Kosovo and would not sign the agreement. The ethnic cleansing continued unabated with more and more Albanians fleeing from the Serb forces.

It won't take long!

'I don't see [the bombing] as a long-term operation. I think that this is something to deter and damage and is something that is achievable within a relatively short period of time.'
Madeleine Albright, US Secretary of State, speaking on American television on 24 March 1999

NATO withdrew the Kosovo Verification Commission (KVC) from the region and on 24 March began to bomb targets in Serbia and Kosovo. President Clinton told American television viewers that the aim was to 'damage the Serbian army's capacity to hurt civilians'.

NATO's bombing campaign

The first targets were air defence systems and armament factories. Three days into the campaign it was evident that the bombing was not having the intended effect. Instead of ending **ethnic cleansing** it actually intensified it. In the town of Pec, Albanians were ordered into the local football stadium and told to get out of Kosovo on foot. They were told: 'You wanted **NATO**, now you can pay for it.' By 29 March over 150,000 Albanian women, children and old people were streaming out of Kosovo to refugee camps in Albania and Macedonia. Men young enough to fight were taken away by Serbian soldiers. By April an estimated 400,000 Albanians were in refugee camps and the international relief bodies were struggling to cope. There was also the threat of disease spreading in the unsanitary conditions. The British Prime Minister, Tony Blair, visited a refugee camp in Macedonia and said: 'This is not a battle for NATO, this is not a battle for territory, this is a battle for humanity.'

Things were not going as smoothly as NATO had hoped. The bombs had not destroyed the Serbian air defences and NATO planes were forced to fly at 15,000 feet to avoid anti-aircraft missiles. The pilots were also hampered by bad weather. Still the Serbs continued to force Albanians from their homes. It was decided to bomb Belgrade.

Several buildings were hit including the headquarters of Radio Television Serbia. There were several civilian deaths and people in the West began to question the wisdom of the bombing. In addition, a number of targets were hit by mistake, including the Chinese Embassy in Belgrade. A train crossing a bridge in southeast Kosovo was also bombed in error, leaving ten civilians dead. At one stage NATO considered sending ground forces into Kosovo to drive the Serbs out. This, however, would have been very unpopular with public opinion in NATO countries and as a consequence it was ruled out.

Buildings burning in Belgrade after being hit by NATO 'Tomahawk' missiles, 2 April 1999.

Peace proposals

On 4 June 1999 the Serbs agreed to accept a peace plan put forward jointly by Russia and NATO. There was to be an end to the violence and the Serbs were to withdraw. NATO would send a peacekeeping force of 50,000 troops into Kosovo (called the KFOR) and refugees would be allowed to go back to their homes. After 78 days the bombing was called off on 10 June. When KFOR moved in they found evidence of atrocities on both sides. About 350 Albanian bodies were found in a ravine and, after revenge attacks began, fourteen Serb farmers were found murdered in a field. Over 250,000 Serbs fled the province and headed for the refuge of Serbia. The war was over but the underlying problems in Kosovo remained.

A burnt out civilian passenger train which was mistakenly hit by NATO missiles in south-east Kosovo, 12 April 1999. Ten civilians were killed and another sixteen injured.

War statistics
Number of bombing sorties by NATO: 10,484
Bombs dropped by NATO: 23,614
93 Serb tanks hit (out of 600)
156 armoured vehicles hit (out of 600)
121 industrial plants hit
23 oil refineries hit
Total cost of the war: £32 billion/
US$44.8 billion

Was the bombing justified?

'Our goals were secured. Serb forces out, NATO forces in, refugees home.'
Tony Blair, the British Prime Minister

'I don't think it worked at all. There is no settlement in sight for Kosovo. We have a large number of troops trying to keep two hostile groups at bay. Meanwhile, Milosevic is still in power next door.'
Julian Brazier, a British Conservative Member of Parliament

A tale of four leaders

Alija Izetbegovic

Born in Bosanski Samac, Bosnia, in 1925, Alija Izetbegovic, a devout Muslim, trained as a lawyer at Sarajevo University. He has led a chequered life being imprisoned for his beliefs by the authorities of the former Yugoslavia in 1946, and again in 1983. In 1970 Izetbegovic wrote a book called the *Islamic Declaration* in which he argued that Islam was more wholesome than either Christianity or **communism**. Twenty years later this book was used by the Serbs to say that Izetbegovic wanted to turn Bosnia into an Islamic **fundamentalist** state similar to Iran. This was not the case but the propaganda was so fierce that many Serbs believed it and many turned against the Bosnian Muslims.

Alija Izetbegovic.

In 1990 Izetbegovic became the leader of the Muslim Party of Democratic Action and was elected president of Bosnia. After Croatia and Slovenia broke away from Yugoslavia in 1991, Izetbegovic said that the country should be reorganized as a confederation, with power being **devolved** to the remaining four republics. No one listened. So he decided that it would be better for Bosnia to become independent rather than face the possibility of being absorbed into a 'Greater Serbia'. He never believed that there would be a war in Bosnia and therefore did not build up weapons or a strong government army. The war and the carnage it brought saddened him greatly. In 1995 he signed the Dayton Peace Accord, recognizing that it was an imperfect solution but the only way to stop the mass killing and **ethnic cleansing**. He was re-elected president in 1996 even though his health was deteriorating.

Radovan Karadzic

Karadzic was born in Montenegro in 1945. He attended a medical school in Sarajevo and qualified as a psychiatrist. At one time he was the official psychiatrist to the Yugoslav national soccer team. Karadzic did not take much part in politics in his early life and, it is said, he mixed freely with Muslims and Croats. This changed in 1990 when he became leader of Bosnia's Serbian Democratic Party and began championing the cause of a Greater Serbia. He came across well in the media, impressing people with his fluency in the English language. Knowing that he had the backing of Slobodan Milosevic and the Yugoslav Federal Army (JNA), he became increasingly militant. When Bosnia became independent in 1992, Karadzic and the Bosnian Serbs went to war against the government and also the Bosnian Croats. He called the Croats 'fascists' and the Muslims

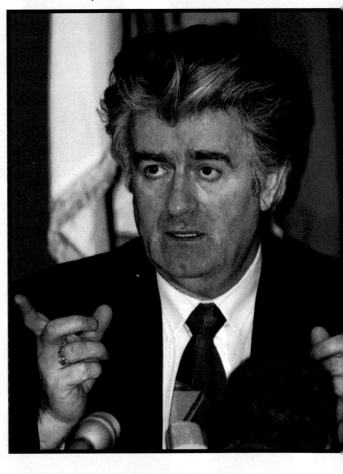

Radovan Karadzic.

'fundamentalists'. Karadzic has been accused of organizing the systematic **ethnic cleansing** of Muslims and Croats but he denies that he was responsible. In 1994, however, his influence and popularity with the Serbs began to lessen. Milosevic withdrew his support for the Bosnian Serbs and then the **War Crimes Tribunal indicted** Karadzic for genocide and 'crimes against humanity'. The international community refused to negotiate with him and Milosevic represented the Bosnian Serbs at the Dayton peace talks in 1995. Karadzic was forced out of power in 1996 and now lives in a heavily guarded house in Pale in Bosnia. It remains to be seen if he will ever stand trial for war crimes.

Franjo Tudjman

Born in Veliko Trgovisce, Croatia, on 14 May 1922, Tudjman was a member of Tito's **Partisans** during the Second World War, fighting against the **Ustasha**. After the war he became a major in the Yugoslav Federal Army (JNA) and then pursued a career as a historian. In 1971 Tudjman was part of the 'Croatian Spring', a campaign to bring more economic freedom to Croatia. This went against the grain with Tito who imprisoned the ringleaders, Tudjman included. In 1989 he became the leader of the newly formed Croatian Democratic Union and a year later was elected the President of Croatia. By this time he had become a 'virulent **nationalist**' and started to persecute the Serb minority in Croatia. In a similar manner to Karadzic and Milosevic he looked for opportunities to advance his own power and influence. For example, in March 1991 he met Milosevic in secret and it is believed that they hatched a plan to divide up Bosnia between them. On 25 June 1991 Croatia declared its independence and there followed the six month

Franjo Tudjman.

war against the Croatian Serbs. Critics blamed Tudjman for losing control of one third of Croatia during the war, saying he had not prepared the army properly. In 1993 Tudjman got involved in the war in Bosnia when he supported the Bosnian Croats in their efforts to 'cleanse' Muslims out of Mostar. After the war Tudjman stayed in power even though his luxurious lifestyle and authoritarian mode of government were unpopular with many people. Tudjman died of cancer in December 1999.

Slobodan Milosevic

Milosevic was born in 1941 in Pozarevac near Belgrade. Under Tito's regime he became a committed **communist**. After obtaining a law degree at Belgrade University in 1964, he had a variety of jobs in industry and business. In 1987 Milosevic became the President of the League of Communists of Serbia and rose rapidly to the top. Within two years he had become the President of Serbia. He exploited the growing surge of nationalism among the Serbs. On two visits to Kosovo in 1987 and 1989 he stirred up nationalistic feelings among the Kosovo Serbs. Milosevic cleverly used the media and mass rallies to get his message across. His initial objective was for Serbs

Slobodan Milosevic.

to dominate the **Federal** Republic of Yugoslavia, but when it started to break up in 1991 he looked to creating a Greater Serbia which would incorporate all the Serbs of the Balkan Peninsula. To this end he encouraged and financed Serb militia groups in Croatia and Bosnia, gaining himself the nickname of the 'butcher of the Balkans'. But in 1994–5 Milosevic abandoned his support for both the Croatian and Bosnian Serbs. His motive for doing this was to get the **UN** to lift sanctions on Serbia. Milosevic's brutal **ethnic cleansing** of Kosovo Albanians hit the headlines in 1999, and led to **NATO** intervening in the conflict. Despite Serbia being heavily bombed, Milosevic stepped up the killing. He was **indicted** as a **war criminal** in May 1999 but, as yet, has not stood trial. In October 2000 Milosevic was forced to stand down after a popular uprising. But no-one is sure if his turbulent career is finally over.

'Milosevic is without doubt the single most influential post-war politician in Yugoslavia after Tito. Indeed there is a strong, rather depressing case for suggesting that Milosevic may leave a deeper impression on history than Tito.'
The view of Misha Glenny, BBC correspondent, 1996

War and the media

War reporting

Teams of war correspondents working for newspapers and television companies covered the wars of former Yugoslavia. Pictures of events as they happened were beamed across the world thanks to satellite technology. This served to bring home the horror of the war and the suffering of people on all sides of the conflict. Reporting from the front line is fraught with danger and 30 correspondents were killed during the war. One British correspondent, Martin Bell, was injured by shrapnel in 1992 as he was giving his report.

In a democracy, traditional war reporting should contain balance and objectivity, but this is not always easy to achieve. Sometimes reporters become emotionally involved in a story if, for example, they witness harrowing scenes such as mass graves. Furthermore, they may not have the full facts about what happened, or they may be restricted in their reporting by editors, politicians and the military. Some journalists have accused **NATO** of deliberately 'controlling' them by only giving them selected information about events. In this way the military and politicians used the media to fight the propaganda war.

One problem in reporting on the wars of former Yugoslavia was that it was an area that few people in the West knew well. It was difficult for television reporters to explain the complex background to what was happening. Events were shown on television but the crucial question of why they happened was not always addressed. To fill this gap television companies made documentary programmes and newspapers published feature articles that explained the history of the Balkan region.

'Best reporters don't always shoot straight from the hip'

'Kate Adie, the BBC's chief news correspondent, told the Edinburgh Television Festival that traditional reporting was now the exception, not the rule. She talked of a culture of sentimentality and emotionalism....implying that she was isolated in sticking to balance and objectivity.'
The Daily Telegraph – 1 September 1998

Martin Bell, a long-standing BBC war correspondent, reported widely on the wars in Croatia and Bosnia. One of Bell's contacts in the Balkans was the Serbian terrorist known as **Arkan**. On Arkan's assassination in 1999, Bell said: 'Of course the man's a killer but I needed access and he provided access, so over the years we had a good working relationship.' In 1997 Bell became the Member of Parliament for Tatton in Cheshire.

Human interest stories

The media often used 'human interest stories' in their coverage of the war. Irma Hadzimuratovic, aged five, suffered terrible injuries from a mortar bomb that exploded in Sarajevo on 30 July 1993. Her mother was killed by the bomb. Irma had serious injuries to her head, spine and abdomen. The hospital in Sarajevo lacked the equipment to treat her so the surgeons asked the media to publicize her plight. The British Prime Minister, John Major, took up her case and she was flown to London for treatment at Great Ormond Street children's hospital. Sadly, she died in her sleep on 1 April 1995.

The story invoked a great deal of debate. It gained massive media coverage to begin with but then faded from the news. Some people questioned why one child should have had such special attention when there were many other injured people in Sarajevo. Others said it was a publicity stunt by the West. However, Irma's suffering did do some good. It highlighted the need for the **UN** to treat the issue of medical evacuation more speedily and it encouraged other hospitals in the West to take in more injured people from Bosnia.

The propaganda war

Each side needed the support of the public so they used the media to put their respective messages across. The war in Kosovo provides a good illustration of this. Slobodan Milosevic had total control of the press and television in Serbia and was able to dictate what they said. Serbian television continually broadcast anti-**NATO** propaganda. Footage of the Germans bombing the former Yugoslavia during the Second World War was shown so as to compare NATO with Hitler's Nazi regime. President Clinton was portrayed as 'Mad Bill' and Madeleine Albright was shown as a cartoon puppet.

Each side published their own versions of the same event. For example, according to the Serbs in April 1999, there were just 50,000 ethnic Albanian refugees 'all of them in shelters, none of them out in the open.' The **UN**, however, put the figure at nearer to 525,000.

A cartoon from the British newspaper the *Independent*, 31 March 1999. Despite NATO's bombing campaign in Serbia and Kosovo, Milosevic continued the ethnic cleansing of Albanians. Here he is portrayed as a butcher with no regard for human life.

NATO losses in Kosovo
NATO version
One F117A Nighthawk Stealth Fighter, one Hunter reconnaissance plane and three US servicemen captured.

Serb version
88 NATO men dead and 32 planes lost.

Both sides tried to cash in on the other's mistakes. When NATO planes bombed a convoy of refugees by mistake (they thought the convoy was the Serbian army), Milosevic transported western journalists to the scene to allow them to take pictures of innocent dead civilians. His motive was to turn public opinion in the West against the NATO bombing campaign. Western politicians hit back making allegations about Serbian brutality. For example, there were claims that the Serbs had set up rape camps to carry out the systematic abuse of young Albanian women. The British even set up a website in Serbo-Croat to inform the Serbian people of the atrocities being committed in Kosovo.

The media on trial
On 29 February 2000 a court case opened at the High Court in London. British Independent Television News (ITN) and two reporters, Penny Marshall and Ian Williams sued *Living Marxism*, a left-wing magazine. *Living Marxism* had published an article saying that a picture showing emaciated Muslims in a Bosnian detention centre in 1992 had been faked in an ITN television report. The article claimed that the image was created 'by camera angles and editing' and that the reporters had put a piece of barbed wire in front of them to make it looks as though the Muslims were in a prison camp. The article was called 'The Picture That Fooled the World' and it claimed that the two reporters were trying to provide a 'sensational image of suffering' so that people in the West would take the side of the Muslims against the Bosnian Serbs.

After a two-week trial the jury found in favour of the two journalists and awarded them damages of £150,000 each. The editor of *Living Marxism* said that the magazine would most likely be forced out of business. A spokesperson for ITN said that taking the case to court was 'the only way of nailing the lie once and for all'.

The aftermath of war

Unfortunately, the end to the wars in former Yugoslavia has not brought peace and harmony to the Balkans. The only country to emerge relatively unscathed is Slovenia where a parliamentary democracy has been established that gives full rights to the country's small minority groups. Slovenia is therefore recognized by the international community and hopes to join the **EU** and **NATO** in due course.

Balkan Headlines

US $1.2bn sought to rebuild Bosnia
(April 1996)

Serb ethnic cleansing returns to Bosnia
(June 1996)

Drunken Croat mob force returning Muslims to flee villages
(August 1997)

The war in Kosovo is over but not the fear
(June 1999)

Homesick Serbs give up nationalist dream
(November 1999)

Kosovo: Is the West losing the peace?
(March 2000)

Ethnic tension continues

Since the wars ended, international peacekeeping forces have been **deployed** in the Balkans. UNPROFOR was originally placed in Croatia and Bosnia, but was replaced by an Implementation Force (IFOR) in 1995 to oversee the Dayton Peace Accord. Since 1996 a scaled-down Stabilization Force (SFOR), made up of NATO troops, has been used in the area. At the end of the Kosovo conflict in the summer of 1999, NATO sent in KFOR to keep the peace between the ethnic groups. Despite these measures, however, ethnic tension remained high and there were numerous clashes and assaults. In the year 2000 Kosovo was still highly charged with tension as the memories of the war remained fresh in people's minds. On 16 March 2000, the BBC's Balkan specialist, Tim Judah, reported that, 'Revenge attacks, bombing and arson have driven the vast majority of remaining Kosovo Serbs and other non-Albanians in Kosovo into enclaves guarded by KFOR troops.'

Refugees

The war caused thousands of people to flee their homes to escape **ethnic cleansing**. But for many it has been difficult to return. It is estimated that 825,000 Kosovo Albanians have gone back to their homes. However, there are still over 70,000 Bosnian Croat refugees living in Croatia and in 1999 there were 550,000 Serb refugees from Bosnia, Croatia and Kosovo languishing in

Serbia. Many refugees are afraid to go back, fearing reprisals from their neighbours. In other cases bureaucracy and red tape stop people returning.

War damage

The fighting caused untold damage to the infrastructure of the former Yugoslavia. Houses, factories, railways and roads were all destroyed, as well as historical buildings such as churches and mosques. It will take years to repair the damage. In addition, there are numerous minefields still intact and live cluster bombs dropped by NATO lie in the fields of Kosovo. Between June 1999 and March 2000 54 people were killed by mines and cluster bombs in Kosovo and a further 250 maimed. The USA financed the bulk of the NATO bombing campaign and says that the **EU** should put up most of the money for rebuilding the region. So far, however, not enough money has been provided. Serbia has been economically ruined by the war and the **sanctions** imposed on it. President Clinton said that sanctions would remain in place as long as Slobodan Milosevic was in power.

Milosevic was succeeded as president in October 2000 by Vojislav Kostunica. Serbians hope that this new regime will be more friendly to the West. Some sanctions were lifted after Kostunica took power.

In March 2000 security forces were still finding live cluster bombs dropped by NATO planes almost a year earlier.

57

The War Crimes Tribunal

An international **War Crimes Tribunal** was set up in The Hague in the Netherlands in 1993. Dozens of people have been named as carrying out 'crimes against humanity' in the wars but, as yet, only a few have gone on trial. It is not the job of the peace-keeping forces to catch suspects and many have evaded arrest. The two most prominent suspects, Slobodan Milosevic and Radovan Karadzic, are still at large. Milosevic, although he is no longer in power, remains active in Yugoslav politics.

Before his death in 1999, President Tudjman of Croatia said that the War Crimes Tribunal was biased against Croatia and refused to release files on Operation Storm when thousands of Croatian Serbs were driven from their homes by Croat forces. There is hope that the new Croatian government will be more co-operative. Thousands of people were emotionally traumatized by the wars, so when cases are heard they bring back memories of the terrible killings that were carried out. In March 2000 the tribunal was told how 'thousands of civilians who had laid down their arms were systematically murdered in Srebrenica by the Bosnian Serb army'. It will be a long time, if ever, before such atrocities are forgotten.

On 13 March 2000 General Radislav Krstic, a Bosnian Serb, went on trial at the War Crimes Tribunal. He was accused of carrying out atrocities against Muslims in Srebrenica in 1995.

Broken friendships

In March 2000 two young Kosovo Albanians, Vlamir and Valentina Haklaj described their experiences in a BBC documentary called, *Moral Combat: NATO at War*. Before the war they lived next door to a Serbian family. 'We used to play basketball with [the two sons] and go to each other's houses to watch movies together' said Vlamir. The two young Serbs were policemen. When one of their colleagues was injured in the fighting they went to their Albanian neighbours and threatened to kill them. The friendship was over.

A peaceful future?

Sadly, the Balkans is still an unstable region. In the divided northern Kosovo town of Mitrovice ethnic Serbs continue to clash with Albanians and KFOR troops. In Belgrade there was growing opposition to Milosevic. In October 2000, Serbian people, tired of the sanctions that brought poverty and misery, rose up against their dictatorial leader. In the other Yugoslav republic, Montenegro, the President, Milo Djukanovic, favours breaking away from the Yugoslav Federation and has adopted the deutschmark as the republic's currency rather than the dinar. It is difficult to predict the future for Serbia and what remains of Yugoslavia. Years of conflict have brought the country to its knees and many people think that things can only get better.

Angry Serbs hurl stones and abuse at German KFOR troops in Mitrovice, northern Kosovo, February 2000.

Appendix

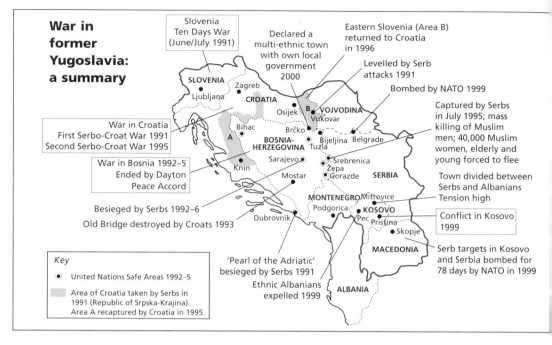

War in former Yugoslavia: a summary

Slovenia Ten Days War (June/July 1991)

Declared a multi-ethnic town with own local government 2000

Eastern Slovenia (Area B) returned to Croatia in 1996

Levelled by Serb attacks 1991

Bombed by NATO 1999

Captured by Serbs in July 1995; mass killing of Muslim men; 40,000 Muslim women, elderly and young forced to flee

War in Croatia
First Serbo-Croat War 1991
Second Serbo-Croat War 1995

War in Bosnia 1992–5
Ended by Dayton Peace Accord

Besieged by Serbs 1992–6
Old Bridge destroyed by Croats 1993

Town divided between Serbs and Albanians Tension high

Conflict in Kosovo 1999

Serb targets in Kosovo and Serbia bombed for 78 days by NATO in 1999

'Pearl of the Adriatic' besieged by Serbs 1991
Ethnic Albanians expelled 1999

SLOVENIA — Ljubljana — Zagreb
CROATIA — Osijek — Bihac — Brčko — Knin — Sarajevo — Mostar — Dubrovnik
BOSNIA-HERZEGOVINA — Tuzla — Bijeljina — Belgrade
VOJVODINA — Vukovar
Srebrenica — Zepa — Gorazde
SERBIA
MONTENEGRO — Mitrovice — Podgorica — KOSOVO — Pec — Pristina — Skopje
MACEDONIA
ALBANIA

Key
- United Nations Safe Areas 1992–5
- Area of Croatia taken by Serbs in 1991 (Republic of Srpska-Krajina). Area A recaptured by Croatia in 1995.

Further Reading

Yugoslavia's Bloody Collapse, by Christopher Bennett – Hurst and Company, 1995

The Fall of Yugoslavia, by Misha Glenny – Penguin, 1996

Yugoslavia, by Viktor Meier – Routledge, 1995

The Death of Yugoslavia, by Laura Silber and Alan Little – Penguin/BBC, 1995

The Serbs: History, Myth and the Destruction of Yugoslavia, by Tim Judah – Yale University Press, 1997

Burn this House: the Making and Unmaking of Yugoslavia, by Ed Jasminka Udovicki and James Ridgeway – Duke University Press, 1997

The Breakup of Yugoslavia and the War in Bosnia, by Carole Rogel – Greenwood Press, 1998

Useful websites

http://abcnews.com
ABC News

http://www.cnn.com/WORLD
and http:///europe.cnn.com
CNN

www.amnesty.org
Amnesty International

www.centraleurope.com
Central Europe Online

www.ssees.ac.uk
School of Slavonic and East European Studies, University College London

www.hrw.org
Human Rights Watch

Chronology of events

AD500–700   Southern Slavs migrate into the Balkans

1389   Battle of Kosovo Polje

1400s/1500s   The Balkans divided between the Ottoman and Habsburg Empires, a situation that lasts for over 500 years

1844   Idea of a Greater Serbia put forward by Ilija Garasanin

1845   Serbia recognized as independent.
Bosnia-Herzegovina comes under the administration of Austria-Hungary.

1908   Bosnia-Herzegovina annexed by Austria-Hungary

1912/13   The Balkan Wars

1914   *28 June* Archduke Franz Ferdinand assassinated in Sarajevo by Gavrilo Princip

1915   *1 August* Outbreak of First World War

1918   Ottoman and Austro-Hungarian Empires broken up

1918   *1 December* Kingdom of Serbs, Croats and Slovenes set up

1919   Country renamed as Yugoslavia (Land of the Southern Slavs)

1934   Assassination of King Alexander I in Marseilles

1941   Yugoslavia invaded by Nazi Germany and its Italian allies

1945   Tito establishes the Socialist Federal Republic of Yugoslavia

1980   Death of Tito

1989   *28 June* 600th anniversary of the Battle of Kosovo Polje. Slobodan Milosevic addresses a crowd of one million Serbs in Kosovo.

1990   *April–December* Multi-party elections in the Yugoslav republics

1991   *25 June* Slovenia and Croatia declare independence.
27 June Yugoslav Federal Army (JNA) mobilizes against Slovenia.
July–December First Serbo-Croat War. Vukovar and Dubrovnik besieged.

1992   *2 January* UN ceasefire comes into effect in Croatia.
15 January The EC recognizes Slovenia and Croatia.

29 February–1 March Referendum on independence in Bosnia.
5 April Start of war in Bosnia-Herzegovina.
6 April Bosnian independence recognized by EC.
27 April Federal Republic of Yugoslavia established (Serbia and Montenegro).
August Detention camps and policy of ethnic cleansing revealed in the Western press.

1993   *January* Vance-Owen Plan announced, rejected in May.
November War Crimes Tribunal starts hearing cases in The Hague.

1994   *5 February* Sarajevo market place bombed, 68 killed.
18 March Washington Accords.

1995   *11 July* Srebrenica captured by Serbs 8,000 Muslim men killed.
5 August Croatia recaptures western Krajina area (Operation Storm). Local Serbs flee.
August NATO air strikes on Bosnian-Serb targets.
14 December Dayton Peace Accord formally signed.
Late December IFOR troops supplied by NATO move into Bosnia.

1996   *15 August* Sarajevo airport reopens.
14 September Nationalist parties win elections in Bosnia.

1997   Kosovo Liberation Army (KLA) formed

1998   KLA and Serbian army fight 'tit for tat' guerrilla war

1999   *15 January* Serb attack on the village of Recak, 45 Albanians killed.
February Rambouillet peace talks.
24 March NATO bombing campaign begins, lasts for 78 days.
4 June Serbia agrees to peace plan on Kosovo.

2000   Tension remains high in Mitrovice in northern Kosovo.
Tension as Montenegro expresses wish to break away from the Federal Republic of Yugoslavia.
5 October Milosevic is toppled by popular revolution after attempting to rig elections. Vojislav Kostunica becomes President of Yugoslavia.

Glossary

administer to organize and implement laws

annex when the territory of a country or province is joined to another more powerful country

Arkan the nickname of Zeljko Raznjatovic, leader of the Serb militia group known as the Tigers; gunned down and killed in a Belgrade hotel in January 2000

autonomy, autonomous when a country or a sub-division of a country has the power to run its own affairs

Black Hand Society a Serbian group founded in 1911. It aimed to drive the Austrians out of the Balkans and to unite all Slavs into a single country that would be known as Yugoslavia.

blitzkrieg German word meaning 'lightning war'. Tanks and planes combine to strike swiftly at the enemy.

Chetniks groups of Serb guerrilla fighters, first formed during the Balkan Wars of 1912–13. Chetnik groups re-emerged in 1990 in Croatia.

Cold War the period of political hostility from 1945 to 1989 between the USA and its allies and the USSR and its communist allies

communism a political system where the government owns the means of production (factories, farms and mines)

coup when a small group attempts to take over a country, usually using violence

Cyrillic alphabet devised in the 9th century and based on Greek script, it is used by Orthodox Christians and has between 30 and 33 letters

deployed the strategic positioning of military forces within a region

devolve to transfer power from a high level to a lower level, e.g. to local government

dynasty a family of hereditary rulers, often royalty

ethnic cleansing removing people from an area using violence so that it will be dominated by people of a different culture or religion

European Community (EC)/European Union (EU) set up in 1958 to promote political, social and economic co-operation in Europe. The EC was renamed the European Union in 1993 following the Treaty of Maastricht.

federal a system of government where a number of separate territories are grouped together under a common central government, while controlling a large measure of their own affairs.

fundamentalism when someone believes very deeply in the basic principles of their religion

guerrillas small groups of soldiers who spring surprise attacks on the enemy

Habsburg Empire large amounts of territory ruled by the Austrian royal family (Habsburgs) from the Middle Ages until 1918. From 1867, until its collapse in 1918, the Habsburg Empire was also known as Austria-Hungary.

homogenous made up of the same race of people

indict to accuse or charge a person with a crime

inflation a sharp rise in the price of goods

nationalism, nationalist a desire to unify a nation of people into one country, free of the influence of foreigners

NATO the North Atlantic Treaty Organization, formed in 1949, as a defensive alliance

Ottoman Empire name given to the Turkish Empire that lasted from about 1300 until 1922. At its height it stretched across large parts of the Middle East, the Balkans and North Africa.

Partisans communist guerrilla fighters in Yugoslavia during the Second World War led by Josip Broz Tito

sanctions economic measures, such as stoppage of trade, to persuade a country to change its policies

satellite a country dominated and controlled by a larger, more powerful country

Tigers nickname for the Serbian Volunteer Group, a militia force led by Arkan

United Nations (UN) an association of countries formed in 1945 to promote world peace

USSR the Union of Soviet Socialist Republics first set up in 1923. The USSR broke up into independent countries in 1990–91 following the collapse of communism.

Ustasha a Croatian terrorist group formed in 1929 by Ante Pavelic. It controlled the Independent State of Croatia following the German invasion of Yugoslavia in 1941. The Ustasha was revived in 1991 during the war in Croatia.

vojna krajina a military frontier established in the late Middle Ages to protect Croatia from Turkish attacks

War Crimes Tribunal a special court set up in 1993 in The Hague in the Netherlands to try people accused of war crimes in former Yugoslavia

war criminal a person accused of carrying out crimes against humanity such as mass murder or rape of civilians

Index